CNUT

BIOGRAPHY

Nathan is a writer, director and performer, whose work has been funded by the Arts Council, toured with the British Council, archived in the British Film Institute and broadcast on Channel Four. His poetry has been published by Dead Ink, Inky Needles, Poetry Space, Manchester Metropolitan University and performed at Jazz Verse Jukebox, Coffee-House Poetry, Hammer & Tongue and Bang Said the Gun. His first collection, *Threads*, a collaboration with photographer Justin David, is published by Inkandescent and was longlisted for the Polari First Book Prize.

Shows include *SwanSong* (And What? Queer Arts Festival), *Foreign Affairs* (Voila European Theatre Festival), *I Love You But We Only Have Fourteen Minutes To Save The Earth* (Soho Theatre), *Flights of Fancy* (Latitude Festival), *Puppetry of the Pops* (Drill Hall), *Guerrilla Gardening* (Pleasance), *VauxhallVille* (Royal Vauxhall Tavern), *Theatre of Therapy* (Chelsea Theatre), *We're Not in Kansas Any More* (Southbank Centre), *Unplugged* (Soho Theatre), *Breaking the Silence* (Arcola), *Femme Fatale* (Wilton's), *The Novice Detective* (Contact) and *Monsters* (Leicester Square Theatre).

Films include *Curtains* (Flare Film Festival), *Rock 'n' Roll Suicide* (London Short Film Festival), *Meeting Mr Crisp* (British Council), *The Significant Death of Quentin Crisp* (Channel 4) and *You Made Me Love You* (BFI Mediatheque).

As performer, Nathan's worked at venues including Roundhouse, Traverse, ICA, BAC, Little Angel, Hoxton Hall, Wonderground and Glastonbury festival. He's principle oboe with London Gay Symphony Orchestra and studied Fine Art at Oxford University. He lives and works in London.

www.nathanevans.co.uk

praise for CNUT

'Evans' poetry addresses vital issues of our time, such as the
environmental apocalypse with biting wit and electrifying passion.'
—MATTHEW TODD, author of *Straight Jacket* and *Pride*

'Poignant, humane and uncompromising'
—STEPHEN MORRISON-BURKE

'CNUT is a kaleidoscopic journey through shifting landscapes, brimming with
vivid imagery, playfulness and warmth – a truly powerful work!'
—KEITH JARRETT

'Story weaving and poetically burrowing, CNUT is a universal backyard
collection of the urban/urbane reimagined, of the domestic/fantastic retold,
of the ravishingly re-readable.'
—GERRY POTTER

praise for Nathan Evans

'In this bright and beautiful collaboration, poetry and
photography join hands, creating sharp new ways
to picture our lives and loves.'
NEIL BARTLETT, on *Threads*

'Side-splittingly funny and achingly romantic. A play about ageing
disgracefully that's ferociously full of life.'
RIKKI BEADLE-BLAIR, on *SwanSong*

'a happy dose of queer cabaret'
THE GUARDIAN, on *I Love You but
We Only Have Fourteen Minutes to Save the Earth*

'a genre-defying exploration of identity – witty, engaging and inquisitive'
EXEUNT, on *Flights of Fancy*

'a high camp attack on high art'
THE GUARDIAN, on *Vauxhallville*

'pure genius'
TIME OUT, on *Rock 'n' Roll Suicide*

NATHAN EVANS

Inkandescent

Published by Inkandescent, 2019

A CIP catalogue record for this book
is available from the British Library

Printed in the UK by Clays Ltd, Elcograf S.p.A.

ISBN 978-1-912620-02-9 (paperback)
ISBN 978-1-912620-03-6 (Kindle e-book)

1 3 5 7 9 10 8 6 4 2

www.inkandescent.co.uk

for Ania, forever

AN ANTHROPOSCENE

OUR FUTURE IS NOW DOWNLOADING

AN
ANTHROPOSCENE

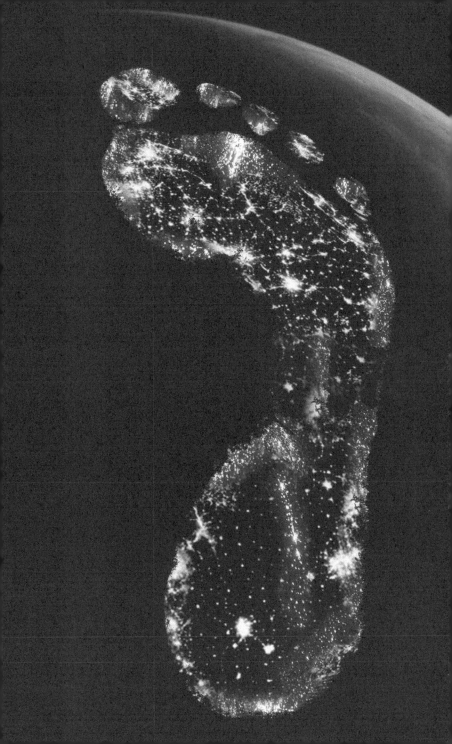

CHAOS HYPOTHESIS

Let the butterfly flutter a wing
Let the double-rod pendulum swing
Let the wicked witch cycle cyclones
Let's get lost in pheromones

Let chaos, that came
before everything, reign again

Let harmony emerge from cacophony
Let parity arise from anarchy
Let new order form from division
Let's set right the revolution

Let chaos, that will reign
after everything, conceive again

GAIA GOES TO THE HAIRDRESSER

Chaos capes her shoulders, *You're sure?*
I need a change, sighs Gaia from the chair.
Catching her eye in the mirror,
Chaos knows there will be more.
Millennium after millennium
drilling in my cranium.
At first I thought it was a teething
problem, then a teenage thing
but now I'm sick of it, sick of it –
my pores are clogged with all their shit
and—honestly—look at me
half of it has fallen out already.

Chaos starts combing;
it's true her mane is looking thin.
But don't you think it's a bit extreme?
She shrugs, *I've tried everything.*
Pestilence? Chaos raises the clippers.
They always find a cure.
Famine? Chaos buzzes the blades on.
They always found an aid programme.
War? Gaia shakes her head,
There's nothing for it but death.
Chaos scythes her clean, comforting,
It'll soon grow back again.

first published by Manchester Metropolitan University in 'A Change of Climate', 2017

PANDORA AT THE POLLING STATION

As lid lifted, winged ballots unfolded,
ascended, misaligned magnets, to opposite
corners, calls unintelligible until
coaxed from the ceiling into a sentence
of which she did not like the meaning
and, wanting to change it, sought
more words in the box but found
only *hope*, stubbornly stuck.

first published by Civic Leicester in 'Bollocks to Brexit', 2019

COUNTRIES DON'T CRY

It had been a bruising campaign –
constituencies weekly-warring within
his body then the Gethsemane agony
of unanaesthetised defeats but as
sun outlined his reconstituted limbs
a mist rose from his gut, condensed
in his throat, battered the dams
of his lashes, baptised him *Hope*.

CITY CICATRICE

The sun pisses its last light across the city.
Pecking its jawline, the cranes look almost pretty.
I shield my eyes, shift focus to foreground
hoardings, shielding another cavity for colonisation:
gold is no longer barred in vaults
but stacked skyward in our streets.

What was once there? A theatre? A school?
I can't recall. The lights cycle
green and I cycle the junction, a synapse
unspanned, a memory unmapped:
if we do not audit our present
how will we know our loss?

BIBLICAL PROPORTIONS
(*or* AUNT SYLVIE'S GOES TO AUCTION)

That would never *have done*: a doorstep thick-spread
with grime, freshly-engraved by the well-heeled
with whom I traffic into a hall now home
only to silverfish, swimming letters
damned behind her door.

In a living room once orchestrated for ensemble voices
only money now sings. A kitchen once calibrated by
figures is blank cheque for mildew's signature.
A garden once fingering skyward in jade
now hides its hands in the shade

of a glass Goliath whose eyes (empty) bigger-than-belly
bear down the back bedroom. The front overlooks
an underpass where Davids dream of waiting
lists (full) and number two, which idles
as a non-dom's nest-yolk doubles.

Half this street was let to us; I'm the last and when my tenancy
(body & masonry) expires the reigning association will let
ruin reach maturation then—restoration outflanking
budgeting—auction, investing its profit in crumbs
from dough-balls proving on our horizons.

DEV THE DRAGON

A dragon called development
now lives on our street –
each day he wakes us, roaring,
each night floodlights our sleep.

His noxious breath precedes him,
though he never leaves his lair –
he's too busy buttressing
the treasure he'll not share.

ROAD RAGE

Ladbroke Grove turns up its nose,
thinks it's a hill to rival Primrose.

At its height, the church preens
and beaks to higher heavens.

Around, a lacework of villas
radiate in ice-cream flavours.

A car the size of a smallholding
Prada-shoulders the cycling

lane, descends past buildings
similar but less certain

(each year their coats thinner
than the well-painted neighbours')

and turns before the nadir,
never ventures there, where

another architecture
elevates its finger.

THEY SHALL FALL FOR GRENFELL

I heard their silence
     before I saw them
          like lava flowing
               past my front garden
                    tacet protest more potent
                         than a piper's summons
                              we moved on the mountain

INGRAINED

we're
gold-topped
cream of the crop
fuelling economies|siloed
in city high-rises| |separate
from chaff and stalk ||| useful only
for patching thatches on piles in the country

WINDOW-BOXED

One March morning, I find my prospect clad
in scaffolding, scrim and a corrugated ceiling
that techno-pounds in rain. *It's just for a week,*
I think, *until they fix that leak.*

April—sage tendrils coil the sill, still no sun
to spring to. May—it advances ambassadors
to the corners of the compass. June—again,
deferments from the agents.

July—a phototropical tangle, unrecognisable.
August—my neighbour (leak not yet fixed)
says she's using a food bank. She's worried
for her kid, drawn up like this.

HOT-HOUSED

Scrolling upon a photo of my front room
(freshly decorated, some years pre-posted)
I'm shocked to see how much you've grown:
status updates overlooked, you're suddenly

branch and leaf above me. When I found you
forlorn, I could read no reason for pavement
abandonment in your upstretched palms;
rehoused, repotted you flourished but

your executive fingers worked close-up magic,
misdirecting my eye from untumesced limbs
while shafting my freely-givens to the crown
and letting next to nothing trickle down.

Top-heavy, you'll topple one day. A tragedy:
floored by a flaw visible only to the amphitheatre.
Nature or nurture? Had I wielded revolutionary
secateurs would you have a full-bodied future?

OLD REDBREAST IS BACK

Look! So cute with his scarlet dress shirt –
he would brighten any day or garden.
No wonder they were voted the nation's
favourite feathered friend.
                              You do know
it's only the earthworms they're digging?
Well this one knows which side it's buttered,
fluttering his wings. Yes, yes. I'll bring some
bread to the table soon.
                              You ever wonder
how they came to be that colour?
                              I heard
it was the blood of Jesus, dripped down
from the cross.
                              More like the blood of
brothers – they're vicious little bastards.
I bet there's more backstabbing in your
back garden than in a coalition cabinet
meeting.
                   Go on, take a picture of me
with him.
                   Jesus must be well miffed,
knocked from Christmas number one –
these days they're gurning from every
other envelope you open.
                              That's going
on Instagram, that.
                              #alternativefacts

DEEP-FILLED

Mince pies
Bellies
Trash cans
Land

SOCIAL MAGNETISM

        encircles

           the globe

                dividing opinion   poles
                            attracting
                  fields of followers
           repelling
                those with compass

       calibrated

    to another north

MELTING POT

after the Felmingham Hall Hoard, British Museum

Unearthed somewhere in England's green
unpleasant land at the nadir of empire,
its cover was raised to reveal Minerva,
sour-faced after centuries stuck between
her father, Jupiter (who could never
resist the sound of his own thunder)

and a supporting cast of random deities
with coarse Celtic accents which, suffering,
she'd come to understand, believing
(as they had in *her* empire) that ideologies
are imported not imposed, until sensational
becomes simply banal.

THEN THE ROT SET IN

Given time and propitious conditions
a single spore is sufficient to fell
a forest. It will settle on some marginal
limb, infiltrate soft skin, stretch a length
to test and—unrebuffed—another, taking
measure of a branch, a trunk, a root
from within, steely spanning until host
is tented and siphoned to its frame.

One arboreal spectre cannot fuel
hatred's hunger. Bridging soil to
a neighbour, it will climb beneath
bark, with leaf handshake take its next,
spread—silent fire—an entire woodland
possessed then, raising bold parapets
above its encampment, broadcast
spore-selves to conquests fresh.

INTO THE WOODS

Macbeth shall never vanquished be until
Great Birnam Wood to high Dunsinane Hill
Shall come against him.
                    —William Shakespeare

Beneath a mistletoe canopy (which lives on tree
benefits but feeds black birds with white kisses)

creatures of every feather and antenna
can shelter in elm or elder;

why then, at the barbed perimeter,
is planted a placard forbidding trespassers?

The storm fells as it pleases;
a solitary trunk is vulnerable to its advances:

this the wood knows and it knows too
that it *shall come against* those that rule.

THE OLD ARE EATING THE YOUNG

in great Goya gobfuls. Don't be fooled
by fingers fumbling for freedom
passes or faces gratefully gathered
as you offer places on buses.
They may look harmless, cluttering aisles
in supermarkets with tartan trolley-bags
but the flesh they're weighing up is yours.
They'll have you skewered and tendered,
torn between dentures, bones boiled
for stock in a big pension pot
and should you dare complain they'll say,
Things were harder in my day.

A NEWBORN IN THE WASTE BIN

There must be some mistake, surely:
they can't have meant to leave me
this way. One second, the dressing womb
then lights, scalpel, C-section and on
without so much as a 'beginners', only
to ascertain my welcoming ovation
was unseemly bottom-slapping. Cry?
I wouldn't give them the satisfaction.

Perhaps that's why, in retrospect,
they didn't realise I'm not dead yet.
Was my breath so very subtle?
It's not so shallow that I can't feel
the Brutus at my back. Oh, outrage!
Oh, indignity! That it should befall me
to strut and fret my hour upon the stage
in a receptacle for used syringes.

Listen! In the wing. I knew it! They return
to gift the greatness for which I was born…
No—hang on—they turned on a television:
the newsreader has quite dreadful diction
and from the matter of her droning
I think I'm probably best out of this –
nothing but war, pestilence, famine…
Death. Next time I'll come back as a fish.

SOLVEIG THE SHARK

—in my four hundred years I've eaten more cold fish than you've had hot dinners—you and all your grandmothers—that last didn't touch the sides—and they're getting harder to find—I go hungry sometimes—not so hungry I'd eat a human—all shaggy skin and scrawny fins—I did try once— when that titanic turd got flushed—gave me indigestion—imagine—an elephantine sardine can cruising the oceans—could see it coming at forty furlongs—can still see the carcass on the bottom—though that's nothing to what you've left on top—islands of it—I don't get south that far but word travels under water—explosions too—ripple our pupils—demarcate our days—I wish you'd hurry up and finish yourselves off—isn't that what you're trying to do—just don't take us all with you—next time we sharks shall rule—

DOLPHIN MADE LOVE WITH MONKEY

bastard child of land and sea, centuries thirsty
we searched our earth mother for paternal traces;
open-mouthed under opaque skies, we gathered
information on tongues, tasted it pooled in ass-cheeks
of leaves until, finally finding knowledge flowing free,
we settled by its stream, drank its oscillating song
byte-blinking in the sun – one-zero-one.

Digits dried in summer and froze in winter
until we dug the channel broader. Now it's a river:
we dam our ears to its roar, dare not swim for fear
we'll be swept from our depth. Soon it will burst
banks, consume camp and return us to our father,
in whose ocean we must learn to live under data,
screened from arctic omniscience by a blubber layer
or squander millennia hungry for terra infirma.

BIRD EAT BIRD

Sampling the stranded spaghetti *von gull*
(plattered on wings that shan't sky again)
our feathered fiend takes no time to savour
its shared genes before secreting them
from a flock flotilla, rippling the reflection
of a city eating its own across the river.

WARN THE COCKLES

Half out, half in, cockle
people ride each tidal swing
but, with black times barricading
sky's rim, must choose between
shore's stony separateness
and sea's salt embrace.

THIS CHARMLESS MAN

When I was young and not yet me, I crawled carpet
crab-like, stood soft-bellied to life's sea, swaying
with its sympathies. Then my first shell was fitted.

I was given no say in its selection but, on outgrowing
took control of each refinement, with pride establishing
the sartorial shorthand embodied in this exoskeleton.

Self-determined, I am island – borders hardened
against oceans of otherness. A sea-lost tongue
I cannot comprehend, or see myself in sun-blacked skin.

BEACHED BALL

at Lady Malcolm's Servants Ball, Bishopsgate Institute 24/6/16

Tricoloured, the sphere sits in a chandelier:
a reveller must have tossed it there,
perhaps the gentleman with upturned
moustache and swimsuit, stripes matched

to the ellipsed plastic perched overhead.
His hands, free, jazz to 1936 refracted
through a 1976 lens—*life's a cabaret old chum,
so come—*

Another forty years on—in London
not Berlin—we too dance decadent on
the precipice of a continent. As DJs segue,
our limbs find release in *Anarchy*

In The UK, tongues in conversation
with strangers on buses home.
If only, we cry, *this folly could be
deflated, recycled as revolutionary.*

THE PLASTIC POPULATION

plastic skins sweat into
plastic clothing churned by
plastic machines ejaculating
plastic semen impregnating
plastic oceans eaten in
plastic fish-gut shat down
plastic toilets upcycled as
plastic sky-fill pissing
plastic rivers drawn up
plastic straws

ODE TO AN ODIOUS FATBERG

Come see, come see, what can it be,
this cabineted curiosity?

Why, it is a fatberg found in a London sewer.
But how, pray, did it get there?

Says here, 'Sluiced from sinkholes, the particles are
separated from water carrier, in blind fear

find each other, join fatty fingers and gradually
cholesterol-chain the city's subterranean arteries

until, amassing critical tangle, they threaten
municipal insurgence'.

Sounds disgusting. How did it come
to be in the museum?

It was 'sectioned and glass-coffined to prevent
olfactory offence'. *Stinks, I bet.*

Close-upping the spectre's Hogarthian horror,
she's surprised to recognise in its spot-lit strata

a pad of privilege, panned casually
and he, a bud of prejudice unthinkingly

flushed, a cleansing wipe-out,
the incidental floss of market

force and other accretions of a
collective myopia.

OSMOSIS

Hunched over a microscope in the biology room,
we saw particles migrating
across a permeable membrane
from a more to a less concentrated solution,
restoring equilibrium.

That was 1989. Bodies no longer cross borders:
the few are building barriers higher
and blocking loopholes
in an experiment which echoes
the distillation we saw in chemistry next door.

FACTS OF LIFE

On your marks…

At the gate, spermatozoa
(ever-eager swimmers) limber,
jostle for position knowing
that when the shot rings
only one may win.

Get set…

Nature recognises
what nurture refutes –
it's most important
not to be best
but first.

Go…

Meritorious millions languish
in navel reservoirs and pubic forests,
to be harvested in tissues,
flushed down loos,
from records.

AN ANTIBIOTIC APOCALYPSO

While doctors overprescribe them
and farmers overfeed them
until rivers overflow with them,
listen, here it comes...

b-BO-boo-boom!
b-bo-BOO-boom!!
b-bo-boo-BOOM!!!
B-BO-BOO-BOOM!!!!

When superbugs don't fear them—
breakthroughs be damned—with even
the simplest surgeon's incursion
will come...

REPEAT CHORUS TO END

MASS MORTALITY EVENT

Microbes with whom we got on just fine for
Millennia are getting ideas: it's too darn hot in
Earth's atmosphere. The saiga have septicaemia,

My deer; they're on their last legs mid-steppe. Starfish,
Melting, wrest off offending limbs and attempt
Escape on just four of them. Fallen fruit bats

Mount up, sardines are packing it in and repercussions
Marley-clank up the food chain towards our
Ebenezer future.

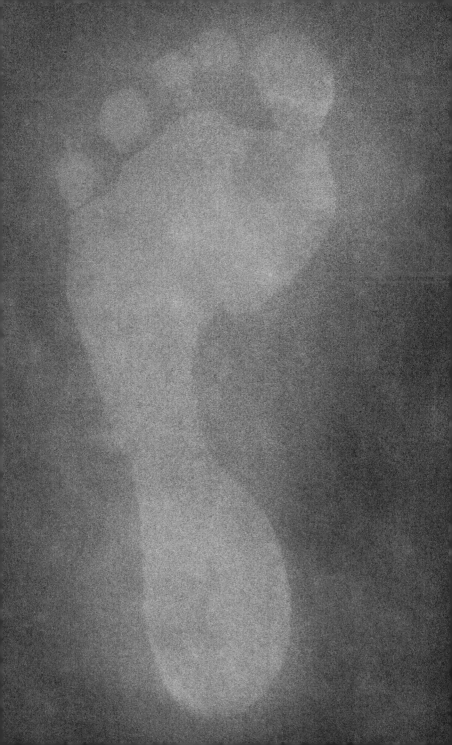

OUR FUTURE
IS NOW
DOWNLOADING

RUNNING IN THE FAMILY

The first time I beat you, or the first time
you let me win, is etched Kent-deep in this grass plate,
so much bigger when I ran in a way that today
I can only imagine, older now than you were then.

Your father never let you win, never came to see you
cross a line. Finding an old greyscale of a *dashing youth*
with medal, I became aware of something in my bottom
drawer I'd not felt there before and (finding it was you)

filed under 'process later'. *You'll always be my son*,
you said when I could not but stand it on my chest.
You'd wanted to garden but had been apprenticed
as electrician, so I must be only what I needed to be.

When I still needed to fit in, I tried and tried for the school
sprint team and was once—to your pride—substituted in.
When I substituted scales for stretches, you came to all
my concerts but were spared all my practise as Tuesday

and Thursday evenings you took my brother (the real runner)
training. Left listening to my reed-warbling, Mum soon joined
you coaching – Wednesdays and weekends, the hobby
you loved becoming unrelenting as the work you loathed.

It was running our lives, you batted on a French green
outside the village to which you'd raced, three-legged
with Mum. We brothers had been coaching her for
a *Gloria Gaynor* after you'd run off with another woman.

The first time it happened, I only remember arriving
in Nan's seventies-green kitchen with overnight things.
You backtracked then; perhaps you would again,
I your broker. *You'll always be my father.*

A TOUCH OF LAVENDER

I thought we might lose you last winter:
the cancer crabbed deeper as days grew darker,
by the time they dug it from your flesh
was octopused about ribs they had to refurbish.

You cried when the dressings came off;
the surgeon said, *I am not a god.*
You knew you would never again
wear a low-cut top.

The branches remaining green with the season;
pincering purplish buds, I inhale a childhood.
The idea came from Blue Peter: I conspired
with a cotton-coiffed grandmother to gather

fabric and fill it with the flower cadavers
you nosed through cheap wrapping paper.
You're never to do that again, you said
and were not to be questioned, not then.

A decade elapsed, smelling out another secret,
you unwrapped it to see my entire identity
had become a question – *why, Mummy,
may boys not make scented dollies?*

These days we drink lavender in tea,
keep it for bees. Yours, bedded,
is tended wearing loose smocks,
mine, boxed, wearing his boxer shorts.

BRIDE OF FRANKENSTEIN

This monster was made together:
her every ultimatum a stitched limb,
his every concession a current
empowering it to grow uglier

until, on consulting her reflection,
she cannot comprehend how,
when all she wanted was affection,
she became this thing bearing *his* name.

MATERNITY BATTLE

Our mothers have been *staking out* again.
Yours has lost her hair and mine
has quite a beard but they're unmistakable
in each rising inflection and imprint on skin.

When first we met, we never dreamt
our mothers would be cohabiting
down the line, inhabiting son surrogates,
fathers in our guts pleading *stop, stop.*

DINNER TABLE TENNIS

Some days we volley forth and back
with a comforting tap, tap;
others (by accident or intention)
one of us disrupts the pattern,
surprising with a spin which may
temporarily halt play.

Some days we start point-scoring
with Darwinian ambition;
others, parameters
are abandoned altogether
and we aim free-form
for eye-sockets, abdomens.

Some days I serve balletically
and you miss quite consistently;
others, it's the opposite
and I have black holes in my racquet.
Today, *all* bets are null –
let the game resume tomorrow.

BRIEFS

Mine sit cross-legged,
yours lounge abandoned,
between them a carpeted
no-man's land.

JANUS-FACED

You're my buttered crumpet
with a nice cup of tea;
you're my mashed potato
with beans and sausages

but sometimes I need
wine and nicotine
to sing the feathers
back onto my limbs.

You're my *Prague symphony*,
my *Roman Holiday*,
my *Rattle Bag* of poetry,
you're my *Namaste*

but sometimes I need
to hear blood beat my ears
and submerge the sub-bass
urge to soar clear.

STREAMING

One hand sought mine, the other, your
song. *I think I might have inhaled you,*
the iPod swooned, *you've gotten into*
my bloodstream.

              I woke to find you
gone. You had an early train so I had
made sandwiches from dinner's remains –
ham (which I don't eat) bought because
I know you like your meat. *Don't forget*
the butter, you insisted, then left them
in the fridge.

             I've not seen you since.
You returned to town. We were to meet.
You rain-checked by text—*drink next week?*
Oh, but the subtext…

              You might have
inhaled me but breathed out again
before you could soak me
under your skin.

             You've gotten into
my stream—45 rpm—until I can bleed
my sound system, breathe my own song
again.

A TUNE A DAY

you are more fretful

than a classical guitar

to play you is easier

a minor arpeggio

will land you low

a major may unmoor
you from the shore
and I should know
better than to riff
on a *diminished* but
when we're in tune
spheres listen in

SOFT-CENTRED

a shell
impregnable as earth
seen from space may smitten

reveal

a molten core that mischievously
spoils waxed moustaches
starched shirtfronts
schemes

THE RETICENT ROMANTIC

Well, you work me:
groundwaters geyser,
glitter in your sun but I can
only tell you this within
the walls of a poem.

WHAT THE CAT DRAGGED BACK

You come home with a gift
between teeth, saucer-eyed

drop it at my feet, smile
Cheshire-wide, sidle up

and purr, *Look what I found
to play with – aren't I clever?*

I rub your damp fur, wondering
which disco dustbin

you picked this one up in
and how best to dispose of him.

CHEMISTRY

At the bar, we follow an age-old formula –
take two cells, apply alcohol and hope for fusion.
If in the morning (should fusion happen
and we head back to mine) I slide between
the panes of duvet and mattress, returning
to wake you with breakfast, do not take this
for an act of love: in time, you'll find
it's quite the reverse. Look closely
and you'll see my mother bending
the bars of my lashes to tell my father
I've been up hours while you've been laid there
and *you'd bring the bacon if you loved me more.*
My cells, after all, are half hers.

DREAMING SPIRES

you
leave
me
in
spires
your
incense
lingers
our worship
sings yet
in my choir
my crypt
once buried
in brick
an uncouth tongue
September-shadowed
and sautéed on pavements
upward-gaping tourists trample upon

THE GLASS-EYED GAZE OF CHRONOS

Compass-less in post-coitus, your phone
peels through pheromone fog, leaves us
ponded in the clock's horizon.
Is it already that time?

We paddle love's shallows a moment more:
I press my lips to yours; you run your fingers
through my hair, reach for shed underwear.
The last train leaves what time?

Dry-docked on love's rim, you consult again
the oracular screen, return to a life dictated
by its digits, omnipotent in every pocket.
See you again some time?

DAYDREAMING IN DETENTION

From a monotone classroom, I project on sky's screen:
in technicolour, teachers are conquered
and I become human through boredom.

A mind squarely-tessellated over life's pegs,
each hour each second sliced and cellophaned
in activity, is clay to authority.

Jump cut and I'm back at my desk—score silenced,
spool snapped—unable to answer teacher's question,
uncowed by cumulus dragons.

PROMETHEUS TAKES A SLEEPING PILL

Pegged to the bed, I wait
for sleep to shroud in night
the hopes and hurts and hates
that peck and peck in light.

STAIRWAY TO PURGATORY

I was running from you, into
a tunnel hard white with headlamps.

Chancing it, I arrived gasping at a gate
then steps, heavy with human traffic.

It was there I met the centurion.
His eyes confirmed he'd been climbing

for centuries. I was only beginning
my journey. Realising I'd not made it

across the street, I wake uncertain
if the city's arteries are still pumping

outside the pane, my heart still
running inside this frame.

DONKEY RIDE

If this is life, well,
then give me hell
and an honest stick
not this carrot trick.

JOY RIDE

Sometimes there is a heaven
and it's just the sun reflecting
on an office block in Euston.

TAKE THE MEDWAY OUT OF THE BOY

Beauty can be captured easily
from the window of a train cross-country:
one may disembark with a pocketful of spires,
a spun sugar river and other confectioner's treasures
but without the bellyache of semi-detachment,
the indigestible decades of deferment.
Even at distance—at high-speed—
those Towns still head-lock me.

BRIEF ENCOUNTER

A woman sits alone on a train –
youngish, I guess from the dress
but can't see a face to confirm this
with her hair and hands in the way.
She could be crying. I look down
at my phone and do nothing:
something is not the *done thing*
on the London Underground.

At the next stop, a headphoned fella
gets on. There's no shortage
of places in this off-peak carriage
but he sits right beside her.
Can't you see she needs space? I bellow
silently, though he's obviously oblivious
to the disturbance in the universe,
let alone that at his elbow.

Glancing up again from scrolling,
I see her emerge from her hair
as he enquires, *You okay there?*
She lost a friend this evening;
I can't hear his reply over the traction
but it appears to be working
as soon she's smiling and dabbing
her eyes à la Celia Johnson.

A few stations on, he gets off, taking
her card. Perhaps, when he gets in,
he'll text and she'll be *fine*;
perhaps it'll be the beginning
of a surrogate friendship or
Rachmaninov-themed romance
—bastard bloom of chance—
which *perchance* I must more.

MUDLARKING

Following the filed footsteps of paupers
past down night's receding bank,
dawn's dull chorus, I see them blinking,
most treasured of tidal-takings:
pennies unspent and bent to prevent
reuse, cannoli-curled and stuffed
with malodorous mud, tarnished
tongues, they speak love's name
to the river's centuries-unturned bed –
Charlotte, Anne, Lucy. William.

History decrees metalwork a male
pursuit: what youth had sanded this last
smooth with sighing, gravely engraved
those seven letters in its surface,
cupid-pierced it, knowing the token
could never be neck laced, at least
not in his own time, and tossed
his love to the Thames, unrequited
as mine. No wader and no shower
can stop this poor skin from stinking.

BLOOD BATH

Now might I do it. Plug in, tap on, write a last letter while waiting. *Isn't that naff?* I shall light a last fag. *Smoking kills!* Not soon enough. *And candles? Why not?* Adds atmos. Then—when water is risen—step from clothing into… *What?* How long might it be before someone found me? A week? *Two maybe?* Calls missed, emails, texts… *It's not like they'd turn up on the doorstep.* But the neighbours might notice. *What is that smell in the stairwell?* Alert the landlady. *What if it was three?* How bloated would I be? *And green.* I wouldn't look good in green. *On consideration?*

Perhaps I should shower in the morning.

TIRESIAS ON THE LASH

Blind drunk may see
more clearly than sobriety.
Stoned deaf can hear
frequencies unfathomable to an abstinent's ear.

COLD STORAGE

Shrivelled, bloated, thoughts sit
unopened, unfinished at the back
of my head, use-by dates long passed
yet I can't bring myself to throw them out.

NON-SINGING BOWL

Fill with water,
bring to the boil,
add one measure
and leave until

fizzing ceases.
Discard contents,
refill, re-boil
and rinse

before re-use.
If only love's kettle
were so simple
to descale.

HEART-SHAPED POCKET

He'll not live long, she heard a midwife whispering
of the child she lay cotton-wooling,
heart buttonholed to breastbone;
throughout his life, he defied expectation.

She peeled a pocket from her dermis,
pinned it to his:
there the orphaned organ beat, blind,
a newborn hedgehog, still soft-spined.

Classmates peered in that breast-pocket,
asked if they might pet.
Some soon learned the citric pleasure to be tongued
in teasing, squeezing; his heart pin-cushioned.

When love's eyes opened, he could not but
wear them up front –
now fledgling, quills feathering, wet-dreaming flight.
His mother wished he were not quite

so obvious as his love leapt into trouser pockets,
got forgot in laundry baskets,
returned, churned, to her familiar fold of skin,
reluctant to leave again

until a neighbour whose own ticker
had run flat called over
for a jump-start. And in his breast pocket
their hearts keep time yet.

A CHILDHOOD ASPIRATION

It had been there as long as he could remember,
sharp-cornered against his sternum's curving:
he'd become accustomed to breathing

life's lows into his abdomen
and keeping the Dolby down
on high-end emotion.

He started coughing,
considered it nothing until delivering
a magenta-marbled epistle into his palm.

The doctor, circumspect,
sent him for tests where his body
was Christmas-party photocopied:

sharp-shadowed on the screen,
was the plastic brick aspirated in 1977
he'd thought never to see again –

a germ of constructed masculinity
that had built its guilt into boyhood vertebrae,
blocking the *unmanly* they said he must not be.

A WORD TO WOODEN BOYS

When you wish upon a star,
be sure you are not wishing
on a defunct satellite or one
of their thousand fragments
rhinestoning earth's orbit for
your dream may ring untrue,
fall clapperless as a cowbell.

GOING GREY

When I was younger, life tasted
technicolour; my palette no longer
registers such vivid hues, recallibrated
to a subtler greyscale of silver,
platinum, slate, charcoal.

CNUT

Put systems in place against it
all you like but our future will download
in the night and, waking, we'll find
bodies reformatted,
minds downgraded,
times shifted.

Thank You

to Katrina Naomi, Kat Dixon, Polly Wiseman
for reading

to Amanda Lyon
for proofing

to Daren Kay
for copywriting

to Gay's The Word
for launching

to Justin David
for everything

Also from Inkandescent

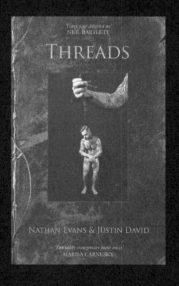

by outsiders for outsiders

Inkandescent Publishing was created in 2016
by Justin David and Nathan Evans to shine a light on
diverse and distinctive voices.

Sign up to our mailing list to stay informed
about future releases:

www.inkandescent.co.uk

follow us on Facebook:

@InkandescentPublishing

and on Twitter:

@InkandescentUK